CABBAGEHEAD

Written and illustrated
by Loris Lesynski

Annick Press

Toronto • New York • Vancouver

For Teresa Toten

(This is when she was little.
Now she's grown up and writes books for big kids.)

We acknowledge the support of the Canada Council for the Arts, the Ontario Arts Council, the Government of Ontario through the Book Publishers Tax Credit program and the Ontario Book Initiative, and the Government of Canada through the Book Publishing Industry Development Program (BPIDP) for our publishing activities.

Cataloging in Publication Data

Lesynski, Loris
   Cabbagehead / written and illustrated by
   Loris Lesynski

Poems.
ISBN 1-55037-805-8 (bound)
ISBN 1-55037-804-X (pbk.)

1. Children's poetry, Canadian (English). I. Title.

PS8573.E79C32 2003   jC811'.54   C2003-900749-9
PZ71

Distributed in Canada by:
Firefly Books Ltd.
3680 Victoria Park Ave.
Toronto, ON
M2H 3K1

Published in the U.S.A. by:
Annick Press (U.S.) Ltd.

Distributed in the U.S.A. by:
Firefly Books (U.S.) Inc.
P.O. Box 1338
Ellicott Station
Buffalo, NY 14205

Printed and bound in Canada by Friesens, Altona, Manitoba.

The illustrations in this book were done in ink, colored pencil, watercolor, tomato paste, chopped cabbage, carrot juice, celery, and potato — wait a minute, I think I'm mixing up art supplies and *soup* supplies — maybe I should move my drawing board out of the kitchen...?

The text was typeset in Utopia and Syntax. The fonts that look like handwriting are called Lemonade and Zemke Hand. The title on the cover is in Klunder.

Write to Loris at Annick Press,
15 Patricia Avenue, Toronto, Ontario
Canada M2M 1H9

Visit us at
www.annickpress.com

Did you know that in France, if you call someone "my little cabbage," it means you especially like them? Kids are all "my little cabbages."

WHAT'S IN IT

Cabbagehead

I need a brain that's brilliant.

I need a head that hums.

I need a head that's ready when

a good idea comes.

Sometimes I'm a cabbagehead.

Sometimes I'm a star.

Always I'm amazed by where

my best ideas are.

sometimes i'm a genius
sometimes i'm a whiz
sometimes i's a cabbagehead
but even when i is
dazzling dreams are going on
new ideas rock
my mind is always mine
and knows
i'll listen to it talk

Hi, Ideas! My Ideas!

I got a good idea,

    then I had another three.

Forty-seven more'd make a genius out of me.

Good ideas

    bad ideas

        some I'm-glad-I-had

        ideas

Come, idea,

    here, idea.

        Whisper in my ear, idea.

        Here, idea.

            Come, idea.

            What will you become,

            idea?

Start one here. Start one there.
Start ideas a n y w h e r e.

one idea

two ideas

bright ideas

new ideas

fast ideas

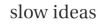

slow ideas

yes! ideas

no! ideas

round ideas

sound ideas

6

weird ideas

found ideas

sports ideas

art ideas

kind ideas

smart ideas

"how?" ideas

"why?" ideas

gotta love them,
MY ideas

I Need an Idea

I need an idea
need it fast
need a good one
that'll last
need it here
need it now
need it fizzing
need it wow
need a
full-of-buzz idea
best-there-ever-was
idea
here, idea!
come, idea!
let me hear you hum,
idea

Think of all the things that other people thought about,
all the good ideas that we couldn't do without...

7

Who Invented Socks?

Every time there's something new,
    ideas are behind it.
Someone took just one of them
    and brilliantly combined it
with just one more or maybe four
    and then experimented,
rearranging all of it till
    something was invented.

All the complicated things that
    came from just a thought!
But what about the simple things
    that matter quite a lot?

Who invented socks?
Who invented shoes?
Who came up with bicycles?
and all the different glues?
Who invented macaroni?
Who invented cheese?
Who invented telephones?
Who invented keys?

Who invented baseball?
Who thought up the bat?
What could I invent today
that's just as good as that?

8

Curious

Do rubber bands melt

if you cook them on high?

Does my blood taste as good

to mosquitoes as pie?

Do ghosts really happen?

Are dragons pretend?

If you ate much too much,

would your bicycle bend?

Does anyone know

where the universe stops?

Can icicles kill you

if one of them drops?

If everyone, everywhere,

jumped up at noon,

would the earth take a swerve

and end up on the moon?

Home Sweet Eyebrow

There are creatures
in my eyebrows.
        They are very, very small.
They live their lives serenely,
        never bother me at all.
I'd never even know
that they were there
        unless I'd seen
a scan enlarged and printed in
        a science magazine.
They look like worms in armor,
        and they never wander far.
You can't believe from pictures
        just how small they really are.
I don't much like to think about
        them living way up there,
families of tiny mites
        on every eyebrow hair.
We have a lot of gadgets
        in the classroom, but I hope
the one we never get is an
        electron microscope.

Dinner's ready!

Coming, Ma.

10

How Do You Fly?

How do you fly when you fly in a dream?

    Charging like Superman, slicing the air?

Spread out as flat as a leaf in a stream?

    Or wispy, like smoke, that drifts here and there?

How do you fly when you fly in a dream?

    Spin over rooftops as fast as a ball?

Or surf on a wave of invisible cream,

    sure as you zoom that a dreamer can't fall?

What do you see when you fly in a dream,

    so far below as you climb in the sky?

When cities expand and mountaintops gleam,

    where do you go when you dream that you fly?

I am
rehearsing
flying
imagining
soaring high
over the city
around the moon
and all across
the sky.
I wonder if by *trying*,
by practicing
in my dreams
soon I might fly in
my everyday life,
impossible
as it seems.

11

Decisions Decisions Decisions

What do you do

    when you wanna be good

but you wanna do something you know

    that you shouldn't,

        oh **what** do you do, do you do?

    What do you choose

        when you wanna choose one thing

    but all of the others are too good to lose,

        what do you do, do you do?

    What do you do

        when it's all up to you

    and it's all so confusing

        you don't have a clue—

        what do you do, do you do?

Have to decide
have to decide
want to do both
but I have to decide
Have to decide
have to decide
want to do both
but I have to decide
Have to decide
have to decide
want to do both
but I have to decide

The Bad Idea Blues

I got a bad idea.
It showed up in disguise.
   It said, "I'm good.
   You really would
be pleasantly surprised."

My stomach said, "Don't do it."
The guys said, "Sounds like fun."
   They all said, "Go!"
   I did, and so
in seconds it was done.

The idea turned out awful.
I wonder what was in it.
   Next idea
   comes to me, I
think I'll *think* a minute.

You can get
a whole lot of kids
doing this one together.
Make up more lines together, too.

Attitude Chant

I gotta lotta attitude
   yes I do
I gotta lotta attitude
   so do you
I gotta lotta attitude
   don't know why
without a lotta attitude
   wouldn't try
I gotta lotta attitude

   — — — — — — — — — —

I gotta lotta attitude

   — — — — — — — — — —

I gotta lotta attitude

   — — — — — — — — — —

I gotta lotta attitude

   — — — — — — — — — —

13

Laughing Laughing Laughing

"The laughter of a little child
  is full of tender joy,
such a light and lovely sound
  from every girl and boy."

The poets writing stuff like this—
  what school do *they* attend?
It's absolutely clear to me
  they've never met *my* friends.

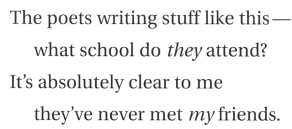

We—
hoot and hiss,
and snort like this,
we snicker, and
we squawk.
We bust a gut, we split our sides
we laugh too hard to talk.

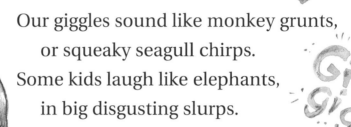

Our giggles sound like monkey grunts,
or squeaky seagull chirps.
Some kids laugh like elephants,
in big disgusting slurps.

When something really cracks us up
we fall down in the aisles,
letting out a howl that can be
heard for seven miles.

Get us really laughing
and this is what you've got:
cheerful, happy sounds, okay,
but sweet and gentle? Not.
Poets need to *meet* us—
they'd really learn a lot.

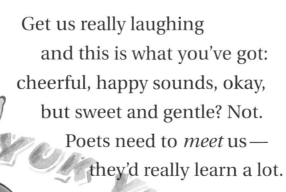

17

The Nibbler

Everybody nibbles on their pencils
    now and then:
a little bite for worrying,
    another nip again.
At least that's what I thought
    until I sat in front of Ben
      —I think he might be *eating*
      all his pencils.

He nibbles on the middle part.
    At first he's very slow.
Then he kind of crunches it and
    munches it. I know
it's likely the eraser is the very last to go
      —the chewy part of everybody's pencils.

How am I supposed to *work* with
    gnawing sounds like these?
You'd think there was a beaver
    right behind me chomping trees!
He swallows, puts his hand up,
    and I hear him burp out, "Please—
      Teacher, may I have another pencil?"

Memorize

Memor-eyes
memor-ears
memor-brain:
my memor-gears
all go so slow
that now you know
why memorizing
takes me years.

16

Walking Past Kindergarten

They write their names in sparkle glue.
　　They fingerpaint in green and blue.
They'll sing a song, they'll have some juice,
　　they'll brag about whose tooth is loose.
And when the door is open wide,
　　I just can't help but look inside
and wonder if a part of me
　　might sometimes wish that I could be
　　　　back there again, for just a day—
　　　　　　but no,
　　　　　　　　I hurry on my way.

PICK MEEE!!!

Every night my Mom will say,
"What did you do in school today?"
I did some writing, I did some reading,
but most of all I did some pleading:
"Pick *meee!*"

"Pick *meee!* Pick *meee!*"
is what I do all day.

"Pick *meee!* Pick *meee!*"
is all I ever say.

Who wants to be the first in line?
Who wants to draw the welcome sign?
"Pick *meee!*
Pick *meee!*"

Who wants to pass the papers out?
Who wants to say what the story's about?
Who'll make the note on the calendar page?
Who wants to clean the hamster cage?
Pick *meee!*

I wave my hand above my head,
but someone else is picked instead.
My arm's as high as it goes, but then
it's somebody else's turn again—
Pick *meee!*

18

Who could erase the board the best?
   Who should collect the spelling test?
Who's got the answer to question 3?
      Pick me, pick me, pick *me, pick meeeeee!!!!*

Somebody, p l e a s e—

            unroll the maps from the second shelf.
            Pass out the cookies (—one for yourself).
            Somebody feed the fish today.
                Somebody star in the harvest play.
                      Pick me!

      I could—
            turn on the light when the movie's done,
            better and faster than *anyone.*
            Tell you the answer to 12 times 4.
                  Take a note to the second floor.
                     Teacher needs someone to get the glue,
                     and **I** need something special to do—
                        pick me!

Finally, finally, finally, hey,
      I'm finally picked at the end of the day.

My hand is numb, my arm is sore.

I hope tomorrow I'm picked some more...
                     Pick *meee!*
                        Pick *meee!*
                           Pick *meee!*   19

Row Row Rows of Shoes

Row row rows of shoes
   lined up in the hall:
what would happen at school today
   if someone mixed them **ALL** up,
      someone mixed them all?

This would be a REALLY bad idea!

Mixed them up
   and mixed them down
      and threw a few away?
         Imagine the trouble
         (in pairs, so double)
            we'd have at the end of the day.

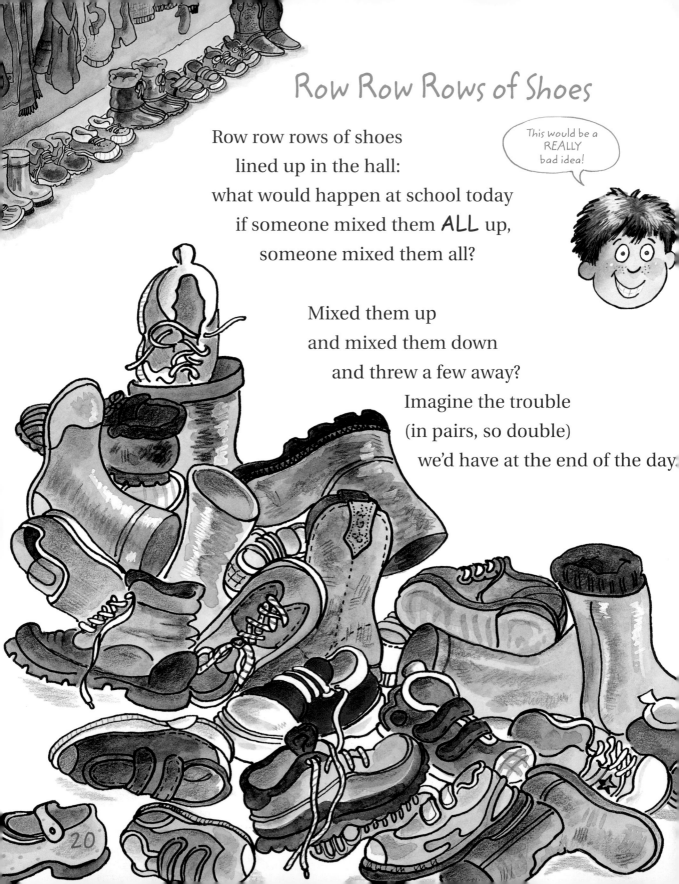

Whose were whose,
the boots and shoes?
    Confused, we'd all complain.
"We don't wanna go
in socks in the snow
    or barefoot in the rain!"

The teachers would choose
who'd sort them out
    as quickly as they could.
Some rights'd be found
on the other side,
    some lefts'd be lost for good.

Before all this happened,
    who'd ever guess
it's a disaster when halls
    are a mess!
Shoes shouldn't be there *at all* unless
    they're lined up
        against the wall,
      the wall,
          lined up against the wall.

The Sweatshirt Lament

The older the sweatshirt
the better it feels.
How come my Mom doesn't know it?
She sneers at the stains,
she howls at the holes,
she says we should probably throw it
    —*out* in the garbage!
    —*out* in the trash!
    —*anywhere* out of sight!
What? When I've just finished
breaking it in
and it finally feels just right???

Hmmm, now I could try a T-SHIRT poem...

The older the blanket, the better it feels...

Dawdle Dawdle

Dawdle dawdle
go so slowly
   let the others rock and rolly
wait a little
ready later
   yawning like an alligator
wrap a shoelace
round a finger
   loiter here and there, and linger…

      dawdle dawdle, take your time.

OR
y o u   c o u l d . . .

step on it and make it snappy!
hurry make the teacher happy!
do not mosey! do not toddle!
never ever! **do not DAWDLE!!!!**

Daydreaming

daaaaaaaydreaming
looks as if
i'm paying no attention
but maaaaybe i'm just
thinking up
a brilliant new
invention.
staring into space, my face
as blank as it could be.
wonder what i'm
dreaming up?
don't ask *me!*

playing with words → ideas

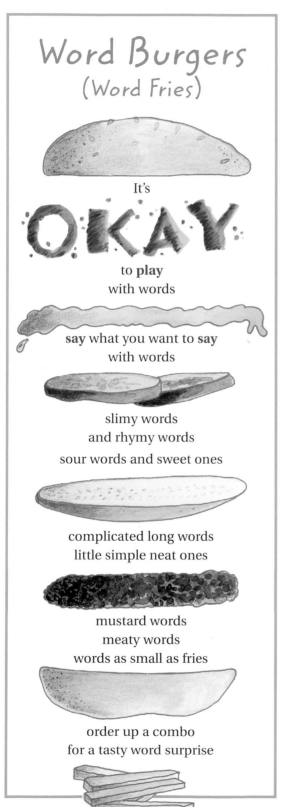

Word Burgers
(Word Fries)

It's

OKAY

to **play**
with words

say what you want to **say**
with words

slimy words
and rhymy words
sour words and sweet ones

complicated long words
little simple neat ones

mustard words
meaty words
words as small as fries

order up a combo
for a tasty word surprise

Nuts and Bolts

Nuts and bolts
mutts and molts
flutts and cuts and klutz and dolts.

Making faces,
faking maces,

po!

Po!

Po tay toe.

Noisy shoes for shoisy news
but newsy blues are
bossy.

I ♥ nonsense words!

I ♥ tongue twisters!

OW OW OW!

Below Below Baloney

Below below baloney,
   above a blue balloon.
Cinnamon linoleum
   and pack a pickle soon.

Below below baloney?
   This'll tangle up your tongue.
Telow telow taloney,
   bis'll bangle up your bung.

    Anonymous asparagus
    is totally ridiculous
    but mangle it or manage it,
      this silly tricky talk

Brain stiff? Ideas flat? Goofy words will FIX that!

gets a brain a-spurtin'
and it says for almost certain:
you'll probably become the
    greatest kisser on the block.

I gotta have rhyme ALL the time.

Wet Pets

What do you call a puppy after a bath?

A soggy doggy!

this is a hinky pinky

When pets get wet,
   they fret and fuss.
They don't like having baths
   like us.

Pussycats, particularly,
   wet at all, are very surly,
hate it how it feels when fur
   is soaking wet, refuse to purr.

Dogs will play in any lake,
   but still, few Rovers like to take
a dip into a soapy tub.
   And birds, you can't begin to scrub.

You will find that your iguana
   definitely wouldn't wanna
take a bath, but loves a spritz
   to wash off all the scaly bits.

A goldfish is the only pet
   that quite delights in being wet
but even so, you know (we hope)
   to never fill the bowl with soap.

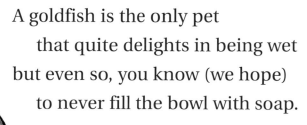

25

L   i   m   o   u

Lim   ou   sine.

Lim   ou   sine.

Longest   car   I've   ever   seen.

Too much gas,

too much road,

always with an overload

of fancy people,

movie stars,

not like us in

tiny cars.

Too much shine,

too soft seats.

s   i   n   e

Drive like ships
through city streets.
What's inside?
More champagne?
Someone with a
famous name?
Windows dark
to hide who's there.
Still, outsiders stop
and stare.

L i m   o u   s i n e.

        L i m   o u   s i n e.

          Weirdest car I've ever seen.

The Have-to-Dooze

Have to get up in the morning.
Have to put on my shoes.
Have to go to school today.
      I don't ever get to choose.

Have to do geography.
Have to learn to spell.
Have to add up a hundred numbers,
      have to do it well.

Have to have my sandwiches.
At recess, have to play.
Have to have a laugh with the guys, and
      a game at the end of the day.

Have to do my homework.
Have to watch TV.
Have to find my book, I'm in the middle of
      chapter three.

Have to do this! Have to do that!
How come I don't complain?
Cuz the *have-to-dooze* and the *want-to-dooze*
      are sometimes almost the same.

Have to do
+ have to do
+ have to do =
The Have-to-Dooze

I ♥ making up words!

A Have-to-Do about Fighting

don't bicker
don't fight
use your nice voice
be polite
teacher said
we have to try
to listen to
the other guy
best advice
we ever had
now go tell my
mom and dad

"Ummm..."

I'll write a book and when it's done
  I'll give my book the title
    Ummm...

Then, a kid in any store,
    when asked what book he's looking for,
  could answer, staring at the floor,
    "*U m m m . . .*"

Librarians would have to say,
    when putting children's books away,
  "Which one's borrowed every day?
    U m m m . . ."

And I *even* might suggest
    that your teacher'd be impressed
  if the book you said was best
    was *U m m m . . .*

My favorite book is Ummm...

Rough Copy

Rough copy hot
rough copy cold
rough copy good or not
five days old

Sposedtobe

Sposedtobe...
sposedtobe...
sounds like one word,
really three.
Spelling just
confuses me.
Is that the way it's
supposed to be?

29

Go Away, Poem

Go away, poem—

    it's the middle of the night.

One good clue is there isn't any light.

Look, I'm in pajamas

    and I haven't got a pen,

and my notebook's in my backpack

    and it's somewhere in the den …

30

Go *away*, poem.

    I'm supposed to be asleep—
something that's impossible
    if you decide to keep
running all around my head,
    dancing on my brain,
sounding more and more excited as you
    make up each refrain.

    Okay, poem—
        I'll get up, and write you down.
Here's a pencil, find some paper
(trying not to make a sound).
        But *if* I'm getting out of bed,
and turning on the light—
    you better sound as good
tomorrow morning
    as tonight.

Story

bits of paper
blobs of ink
lots of squiggles
who would think
that once i got
a decent start
all of it
becomes a part
of a story so good
a story so fine
i almost can't believe
it's mine

Jazzy Cabbage
Tongue Twister

a fridge that's full of cabbage

just to put in cabbage porridge

means a lot of mushy cabbage

that should go into the garbage

and a cabbage jelly sandwich

could not ever be delicious

so you know that no one wishes

for a batch of cabbage fudge.

but... if... you...

camouflaged a cabbage

in a lot of jokey language

on a page of
cabbage poems

... you'd enjoy it very mudge!